# Nauṭankī Folk Theatre of Rajasthan

Meena Ramnarayan

First Printing, 2017

ISBN - 9781726609401

Author Name: Meena Ramnarayan

Book Title: **Nauṭankī Folk Theatre of Rajasthan**

Copyright © 2018; Meena Ramnarayan

No part of this publication may be reproduced; stored in a retrieval system; or transmitted; in any form or by means electronic; mechanical, photocopying; or otherwise; without prior written permission of the Author; except for the use of brief quotations in a book review. Requests for permission should be addressed to Dr. R. N. Meena ([meenajnu@gmail.com](meenajnu@gmail.com)):

## Dedicated to:::

My my parents

Shri Suraj mal Meena

&

Smt: Sumankali Meena

# Nauṭankī Folk Theatre of Rajasthan

Rajasthan is located in the northwestern part of the country. Being a geographically largest state of India, the state has an area of 132,140 square miles (342,239 Square Kilometers) where people live with verity of cultural thoughts. Many saying are famous regarding this area that *'Kośa kośa para badale pāni, cāra kośa para vāni'*, *'Rangīlā Rajasthan[1]' Albelā Rajasthan[2]*

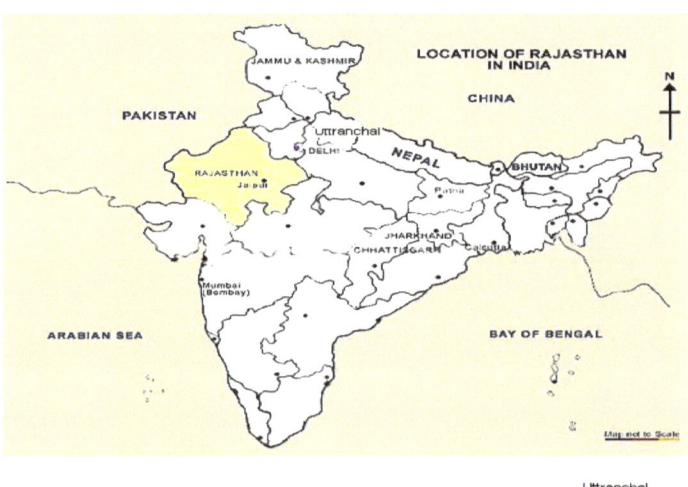

(Map:01; Location of Rajasthan state in India (Source: http://rajasthan.gov.in/District/Pages/DistrictProfile.aspx)

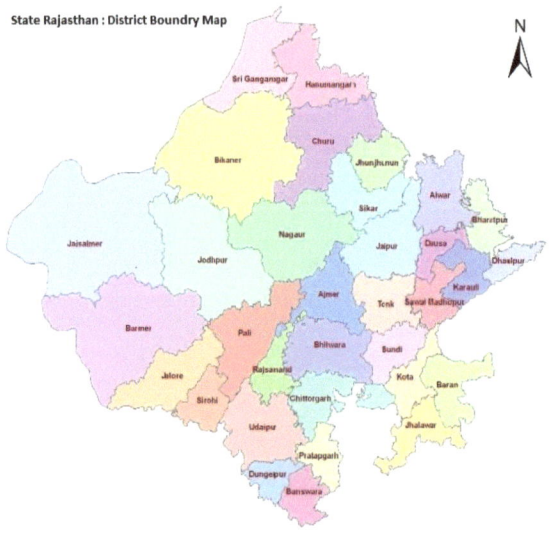

(Map:02, District Map of Rajasthan (Source:http://rajasthan.gov.in/StateProfile/Pages/Geography.aspx, retrieved on 07/05/2015)

---

[1] Colourful State
[2] Different Rajasthan (Diifferent Charactristic)

Rajasthan has a very long tradition of folk theatre. *Rāsa-līlā (Rāma-līlā and Kṛishana-līlā), Ghūmara, Gavarī, Tamāśā, Bhavāī, Swānga, baharūpiyā, Khayāla, Kaṭhpūtali,* etc. are the different form of the Rajasthani theatre which make Rajasthan as a culturally rich and colorful state.

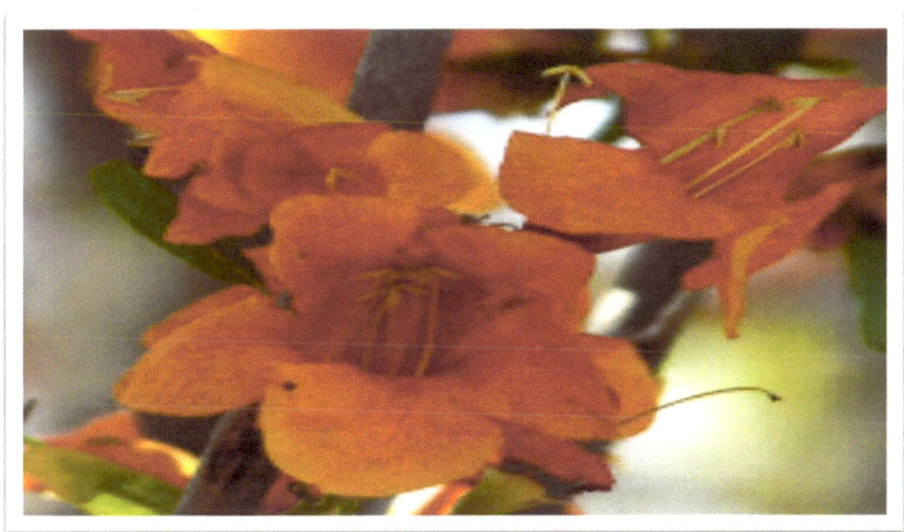

***Image.03 State Flower of Rajasthan***
Rohiḍā (Tecomella undulata) is the official state Flower of Rajasthan.

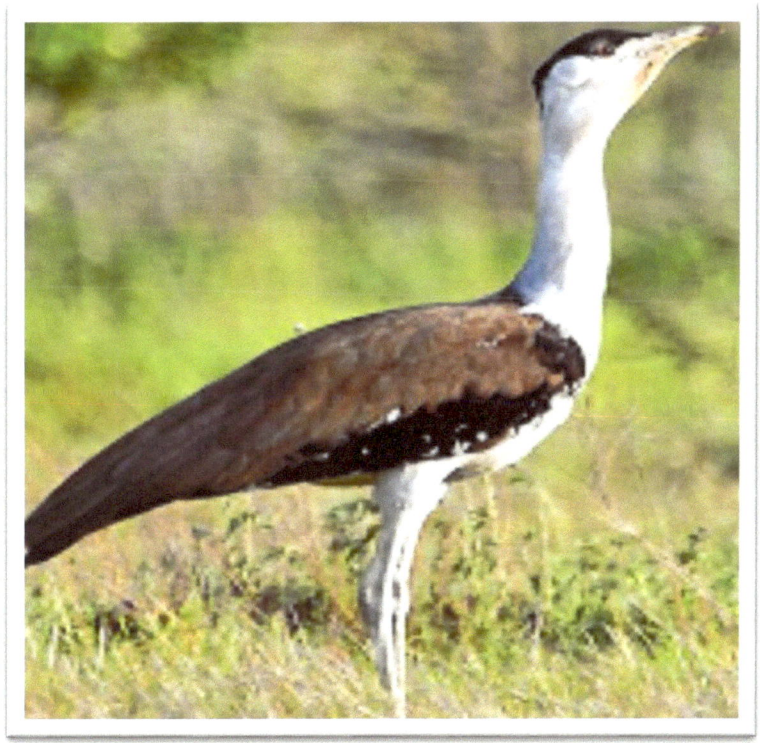

***Imge:04 State Bird of Rajasthan***
Goḍāwaṇa or Great Indian Bustard is the official state bird of Rajasthan.

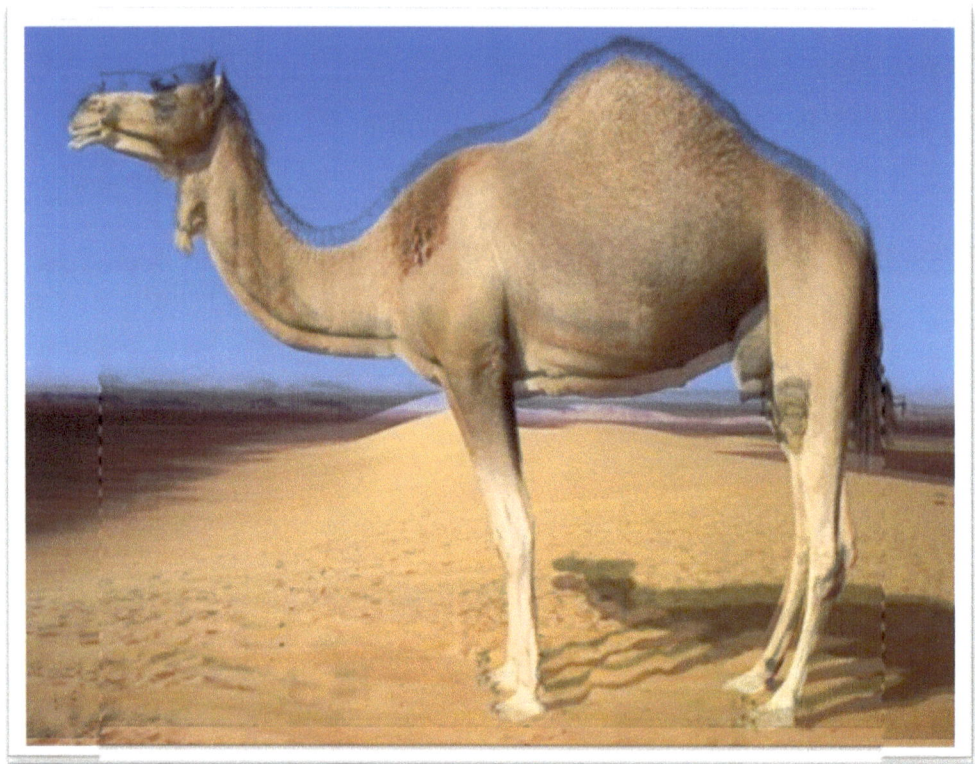

*Image: 05 State Animal of Rajasthan*
Camel is the official state Animal of Rajasthan.

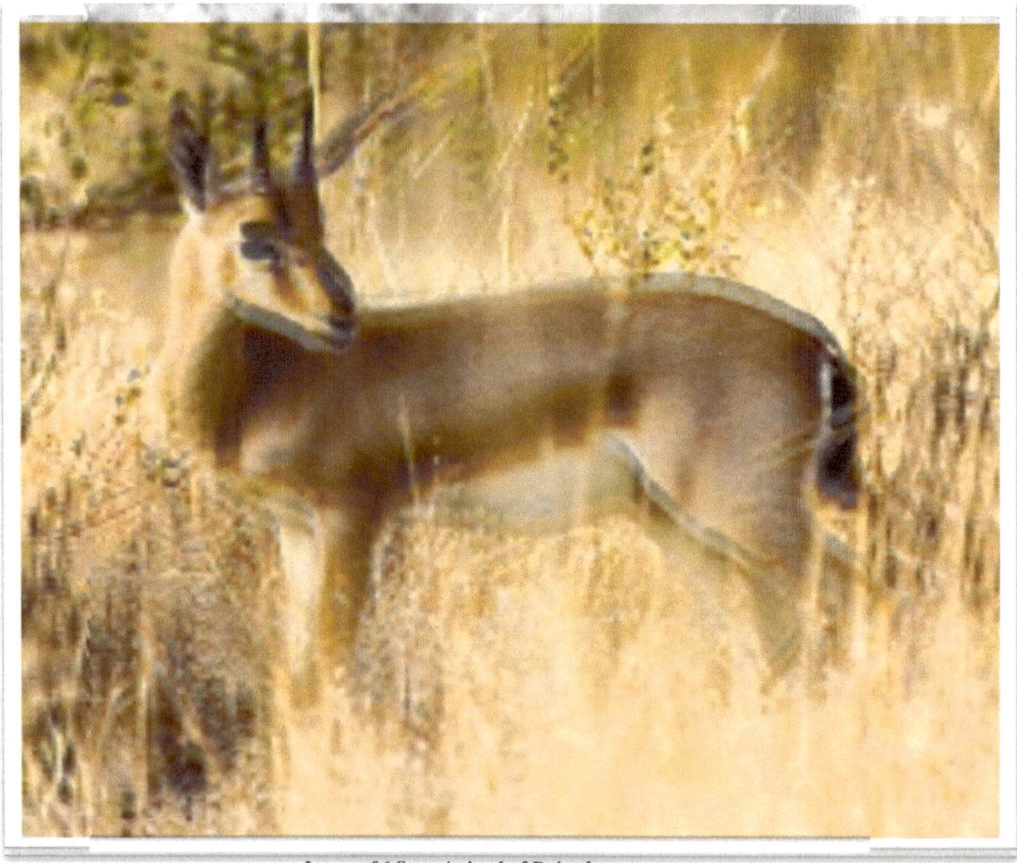

*Image: 06 State Animal of Rajasthan*
Cinkārā is the official state Animal of Rajasthan.

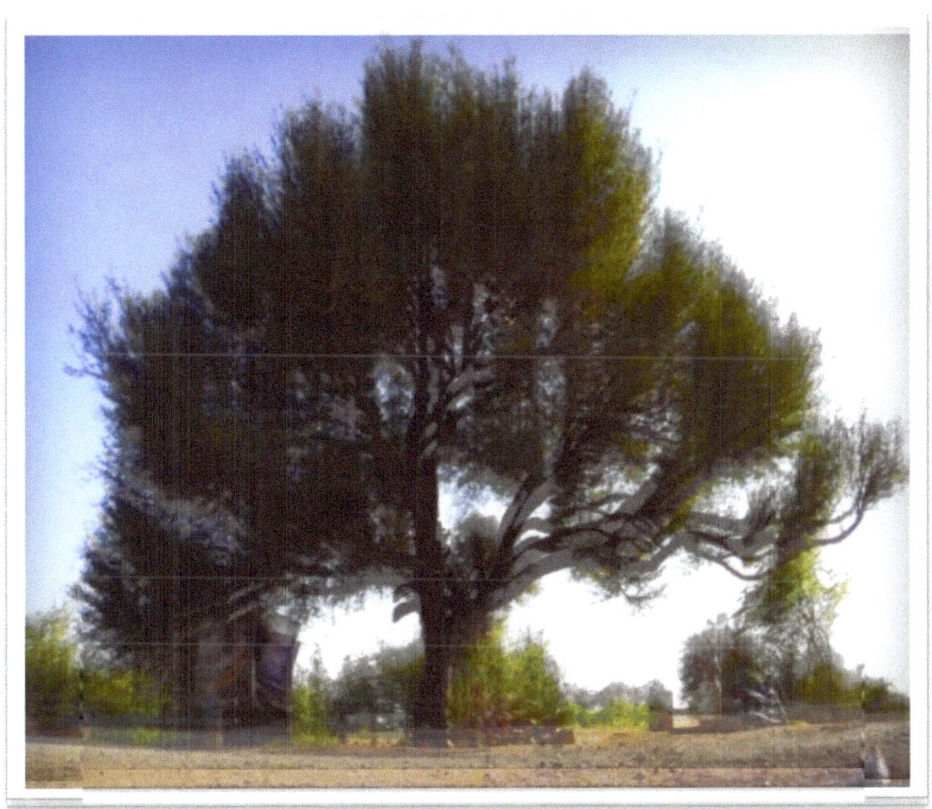

*Image: 07State Tree of Rajasthan*

Khejrī (Prosopis Cineraria) is the official tree of Rajasthan State.

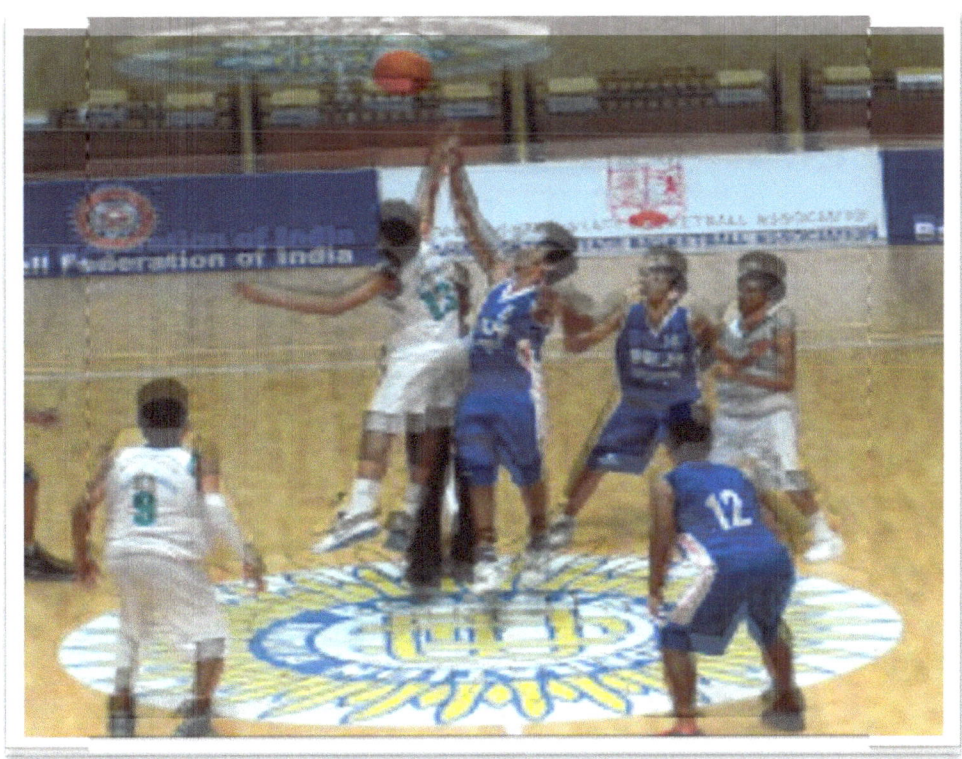

**Image: 08State Game of Rajasthan**

Basketball is the official game of the Rajasthan

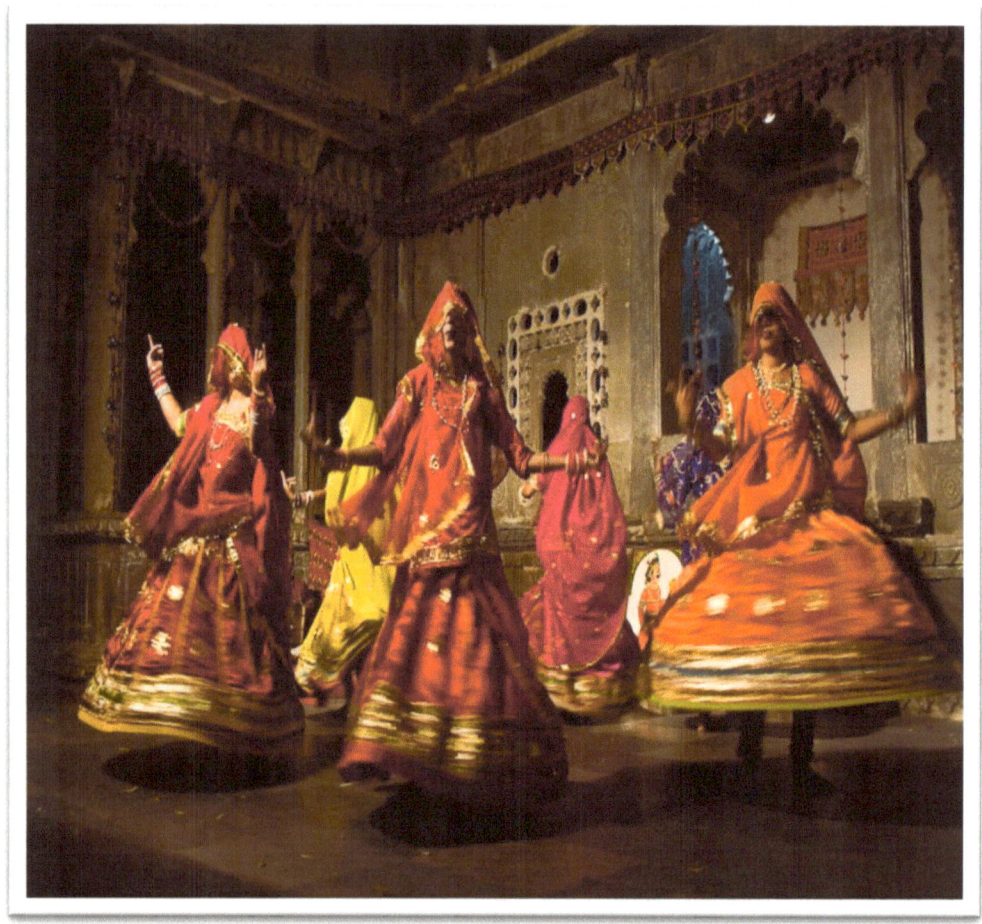

*Image:09 State Dance of Rajasthan*
Ghūmara is the official dance of Rajasthan State.
(All images are taken from https://rajasthan.gov.in/AboutRajasthan/StateSymbols/Pages/default.aspx;
accessed on 13.07.2016)

## Nauṭankī Folk Theatre

Nauṭankī theatrical form can be traced back to the late nineteenth century in the region around Delhi and from here this style of folk theatre spread over from Rajasthan to Bihar covering all northern region of the country. Thus, it is also the popular folk theatre of Rajasthan.

1. **NauṭankI play " Laila-Majanu"**

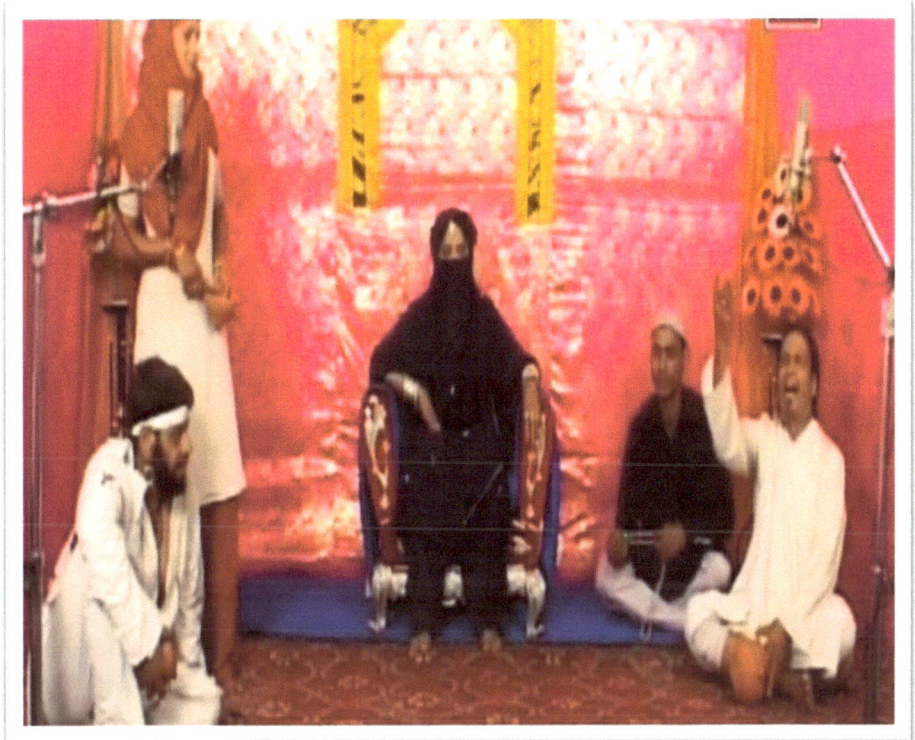

*(Figure:10 NauṭankI play " Laila-Majanu" Directed by Md.Ashif Ali (Source:* The photograph developed from the video retrieved on 11/03/2016 fromthe web pagehttp://hooz.pk/watch/xYyh62mcHLU)

2. **Naṭankī play " Amara Siṁha Rāṭhora"**

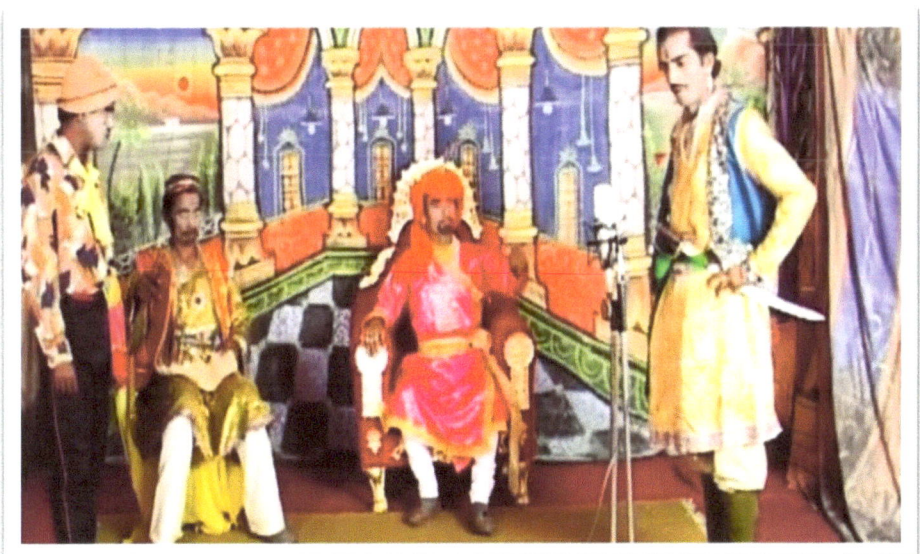

*(Figure:11 Naṭankī play " Amara Siṁha Rāṭhora" (Source:* The photograph developed from the video retrieved on 11/03/2016 fromthe-web-page:http://hooz.pk/watch/eXdjRz6h5vU)

3. Nauṭankī play " Rājā Gopī Chand"

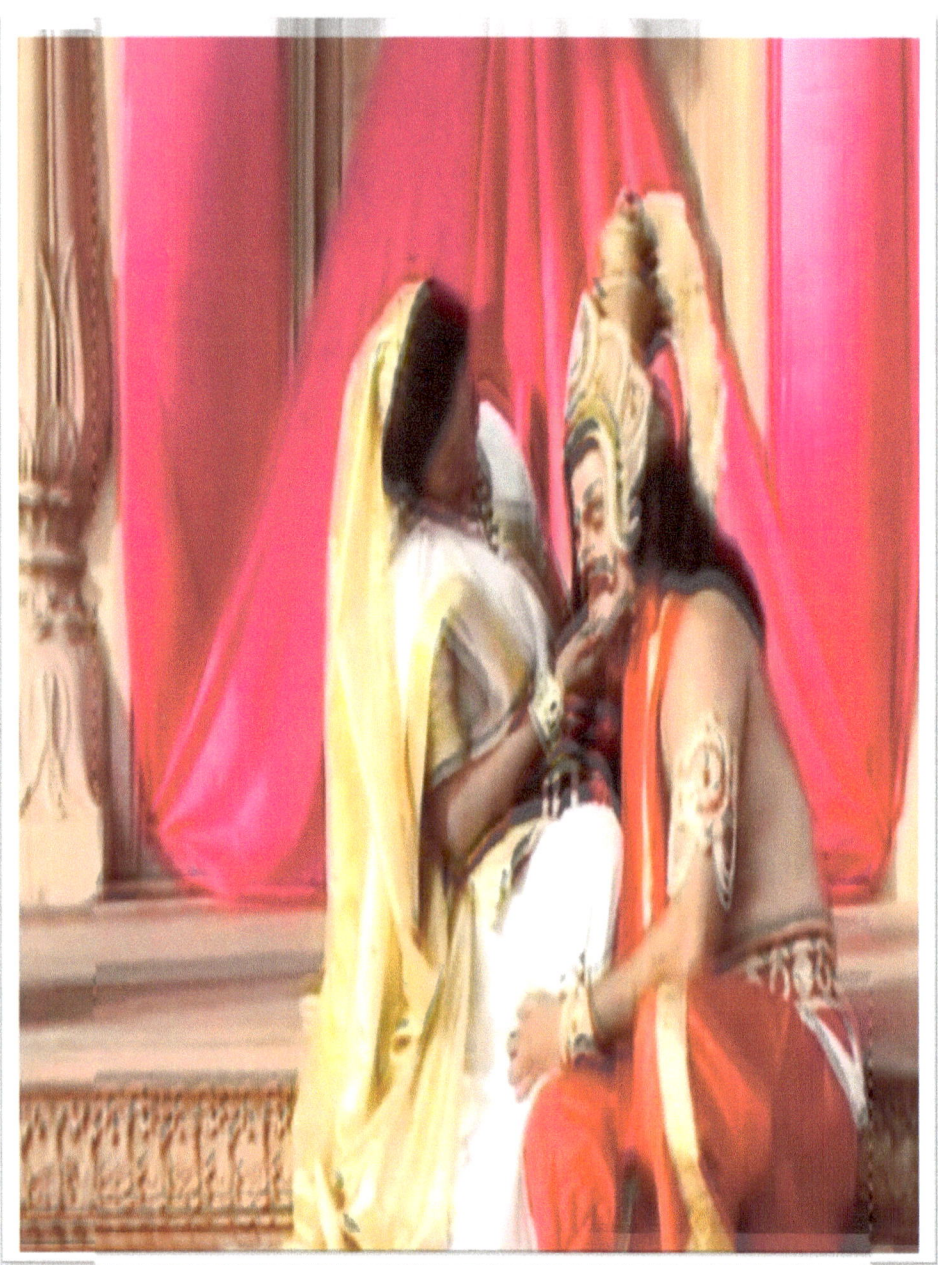

Figure:12 Nauṭankī play " Rājā Gopī Chand" (Source: The photograph developed from the video retrieved on 11/03/2016 fromthe web page: http://hooz.pk/watch/WkiRxKPo9dw )

4. Nauṭankī play " Kīcaka vadha"

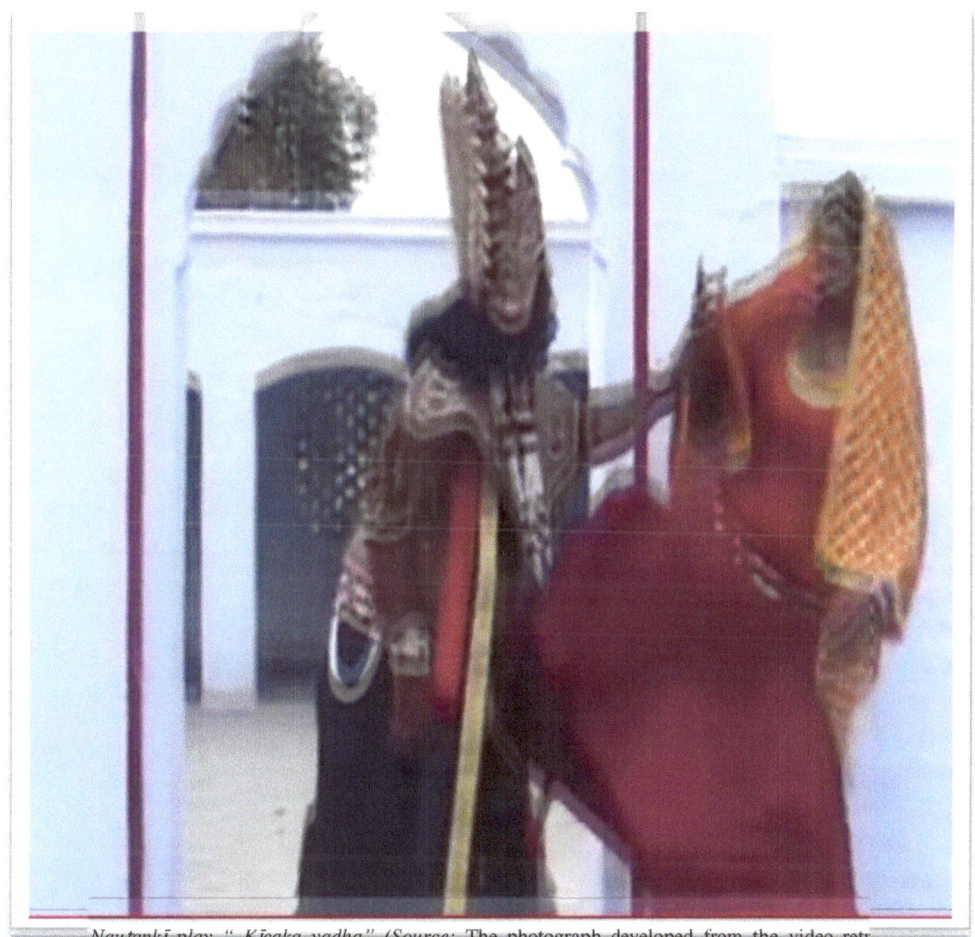

(Figure13 Nauṭankī play " Kīcaka vadha" (Source: The photograph developed from the video retrieved on 17/03/2016 fromthe web page: http://hooz.pk/watch/WkiRxKPo9dw)

Historically this style is related to the Saṁgīta, Bhagat and svāṅga musical folk theatre. Its origin can also be traced from the ballads and bards recitals. When Bards singing their stories, they also gesticulated and dramatized according to the characters. Like other folk theatres, Artist of Nauṭankī should have both singing and acting qualities. The artist of Nauṭankī uses dohā.

## 5. Nauṭankī play " Bhakt Pūraṇamala"

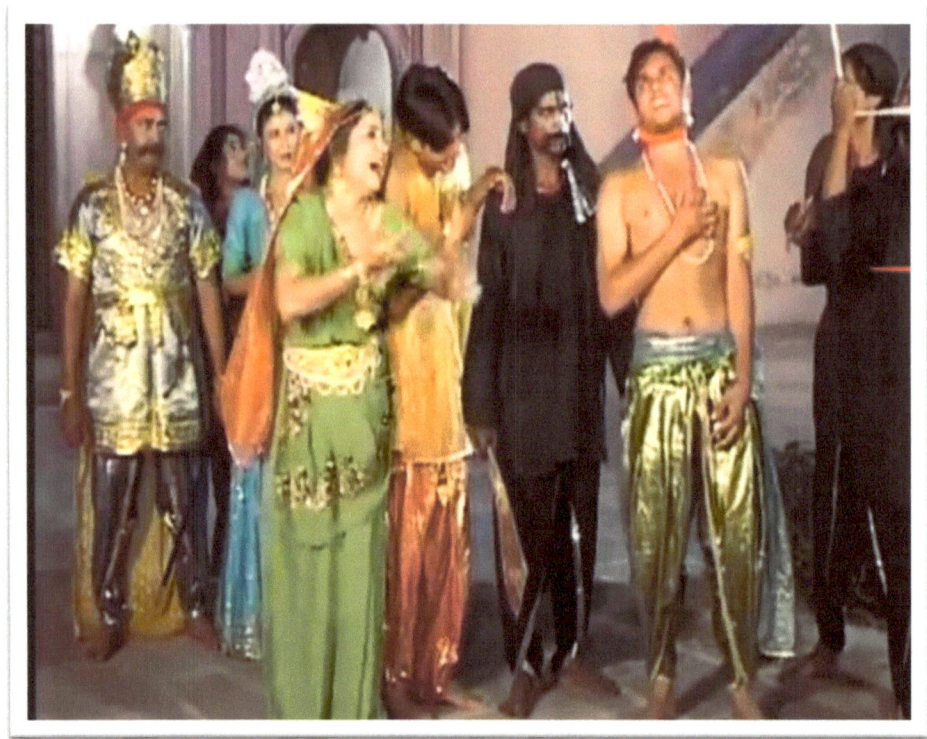

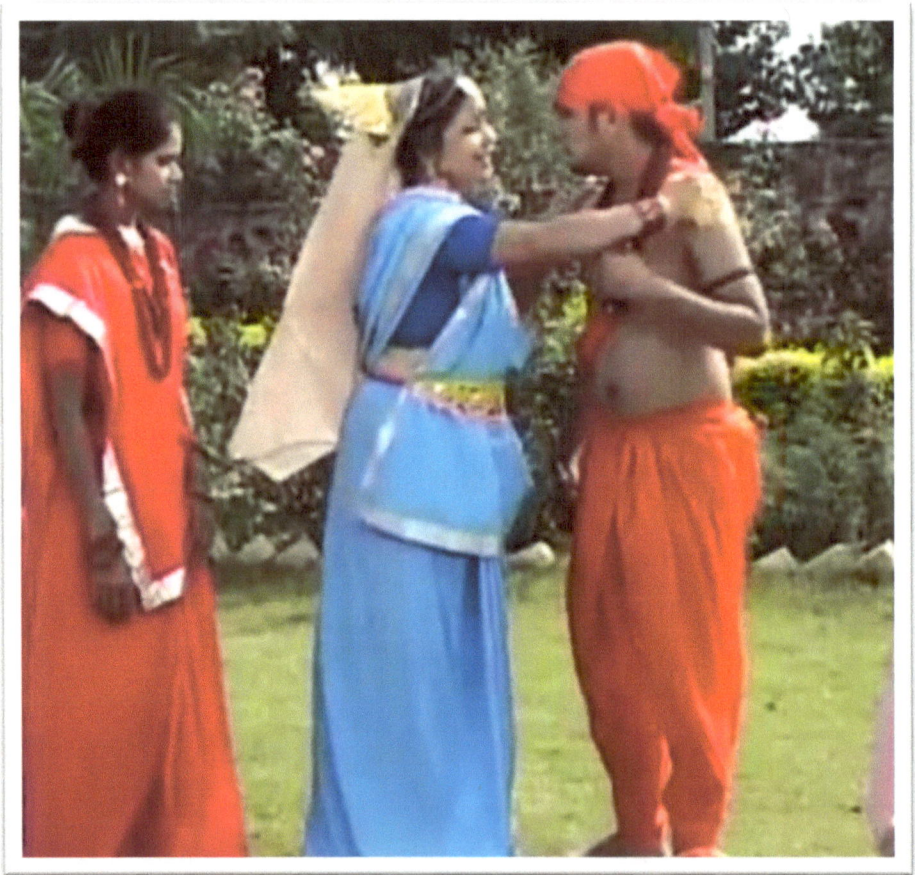

*(Figure:14-15 Nauṭankī play " Bhakt Pūraṇamala" (Source:* The photograph developed from the video retrieved on 17/03/2016 fromthe web page: http://hooz.pk/watch/phCz09887SM )

## 6. Nauṭankī play "Satī Anusūyā"

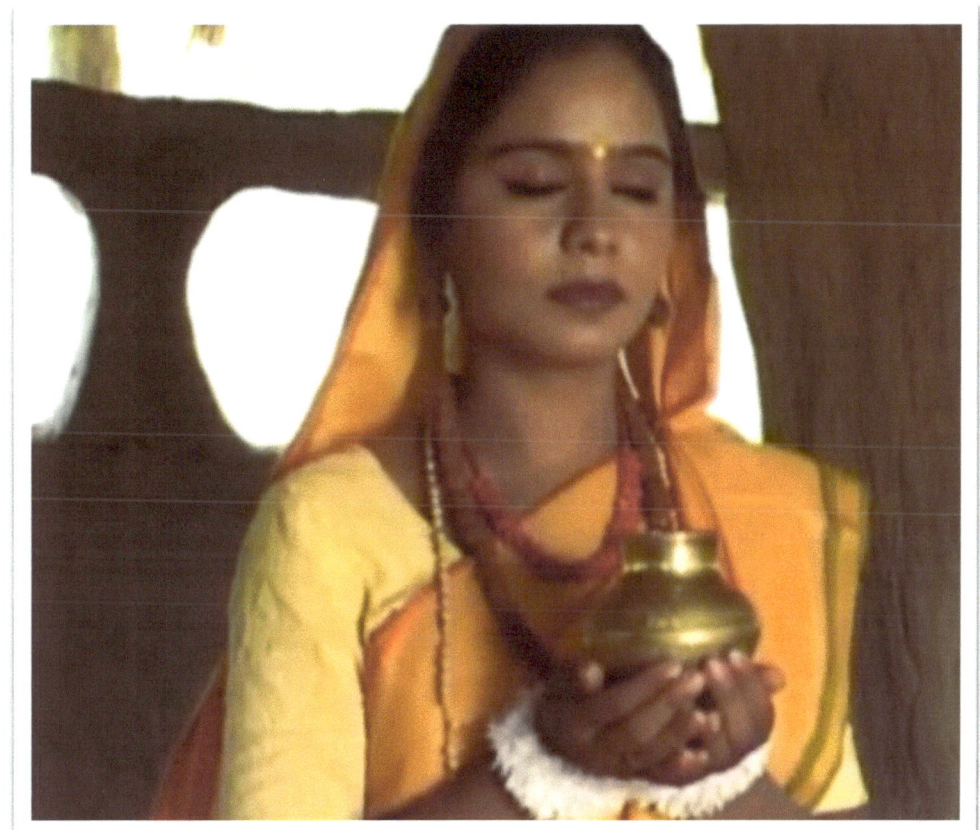

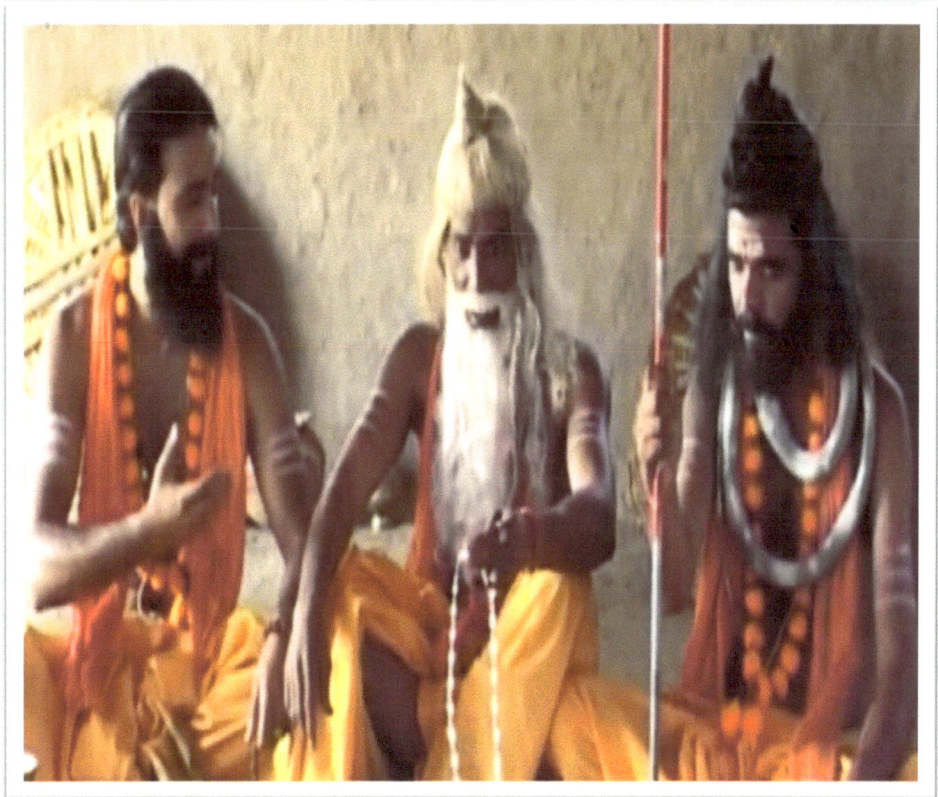

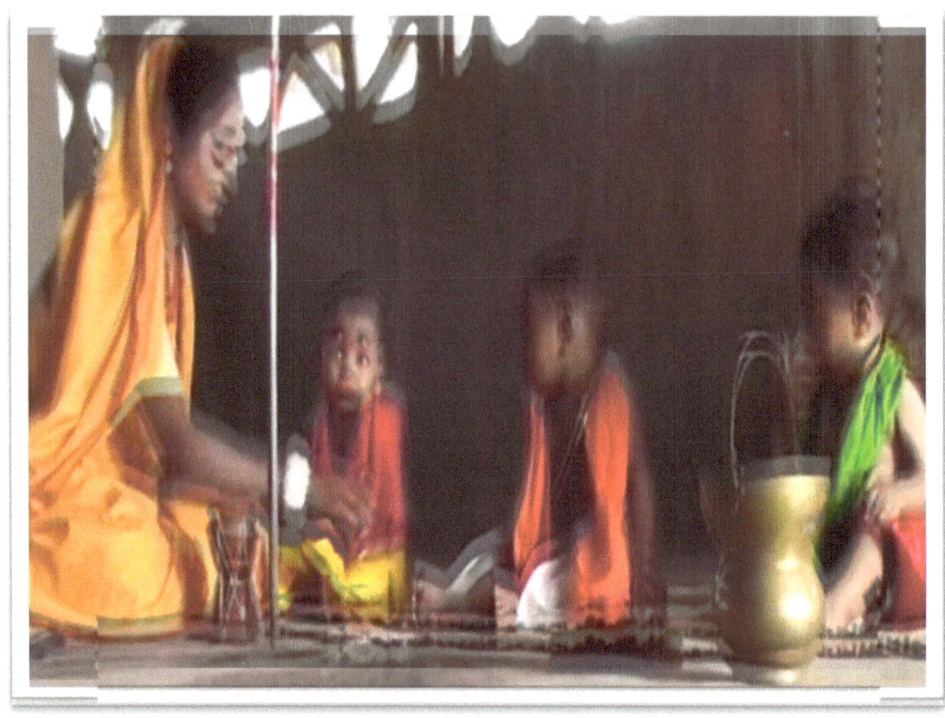

*Figure:16-18 Nauṭankī play "**Satī Anusūyā**" (Source:* The photograph developed from the video retrieved on 17/03/2016 fromthe web page: http://hooz.pk/watch/OE06o7A6JsQ )

## Eminent Artist of Nauṭankī Folk Theatre

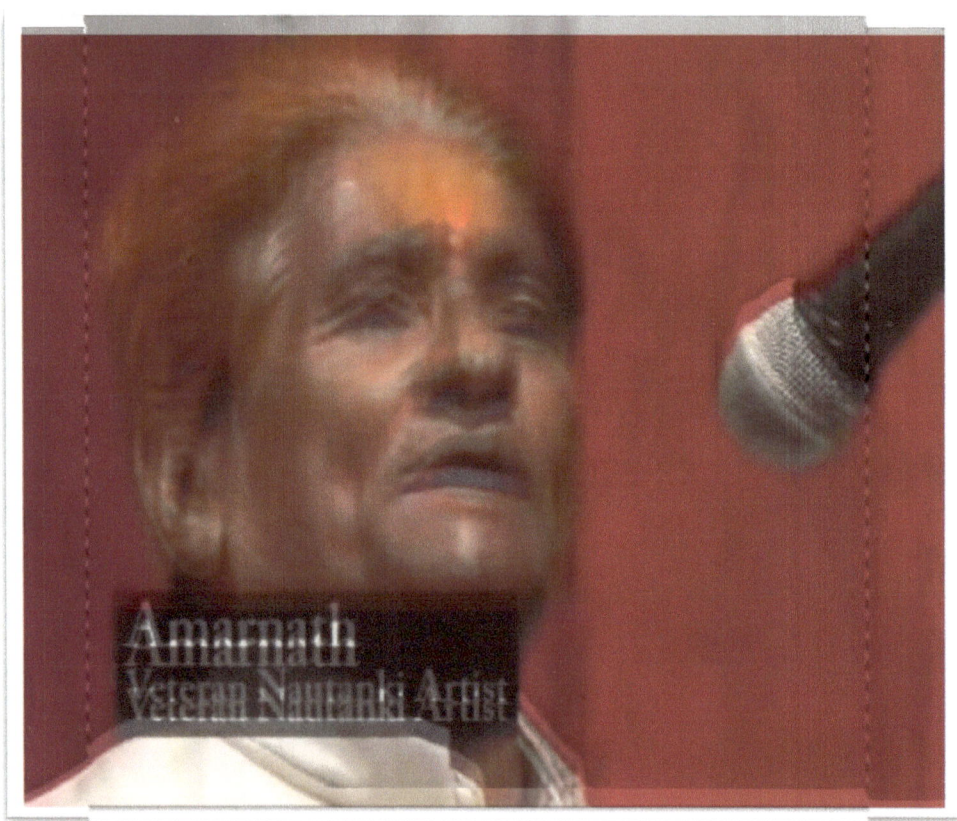

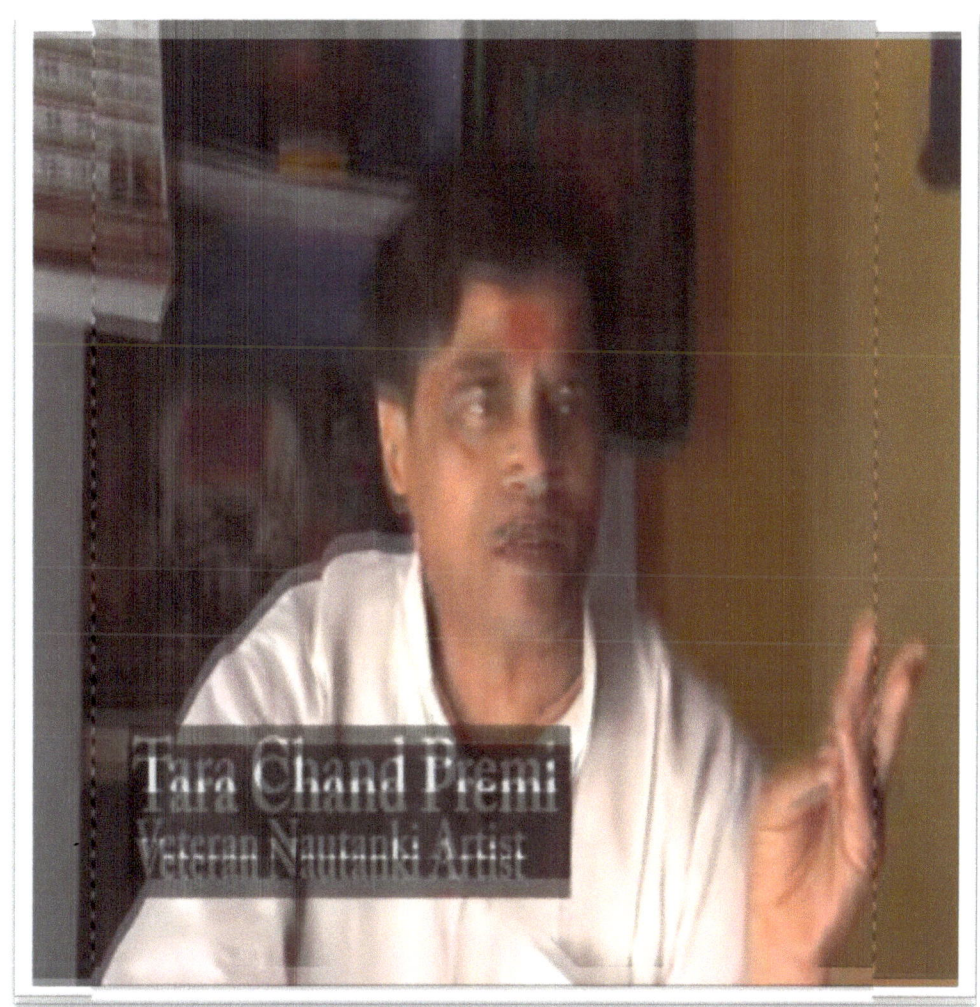
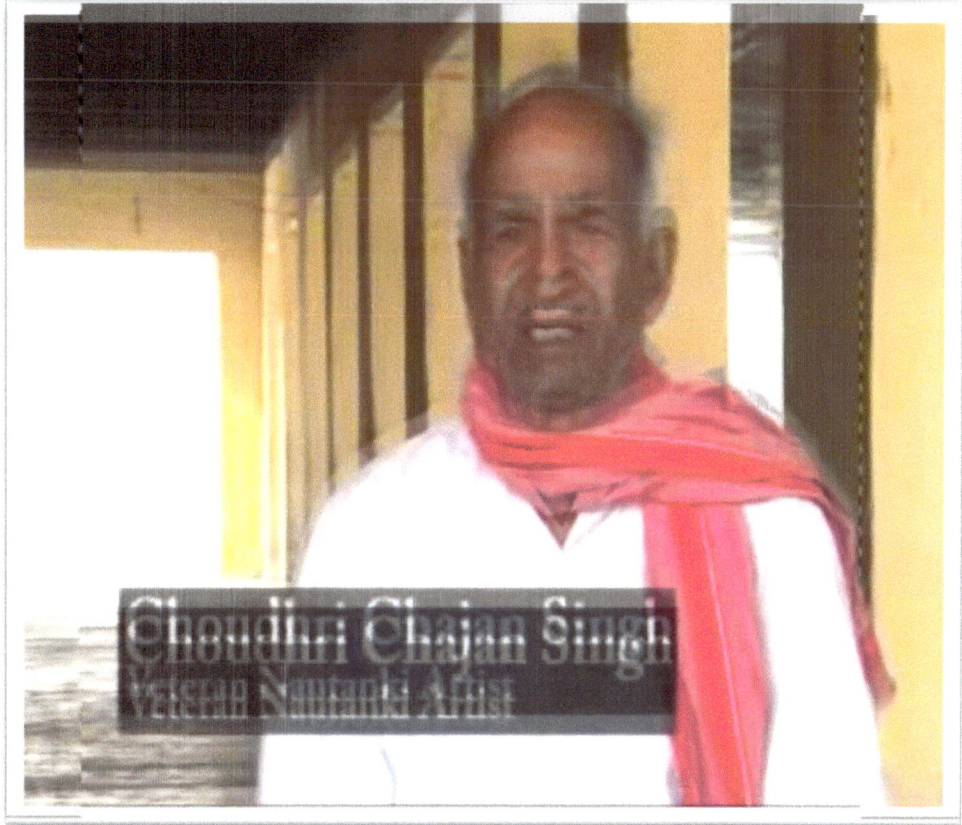

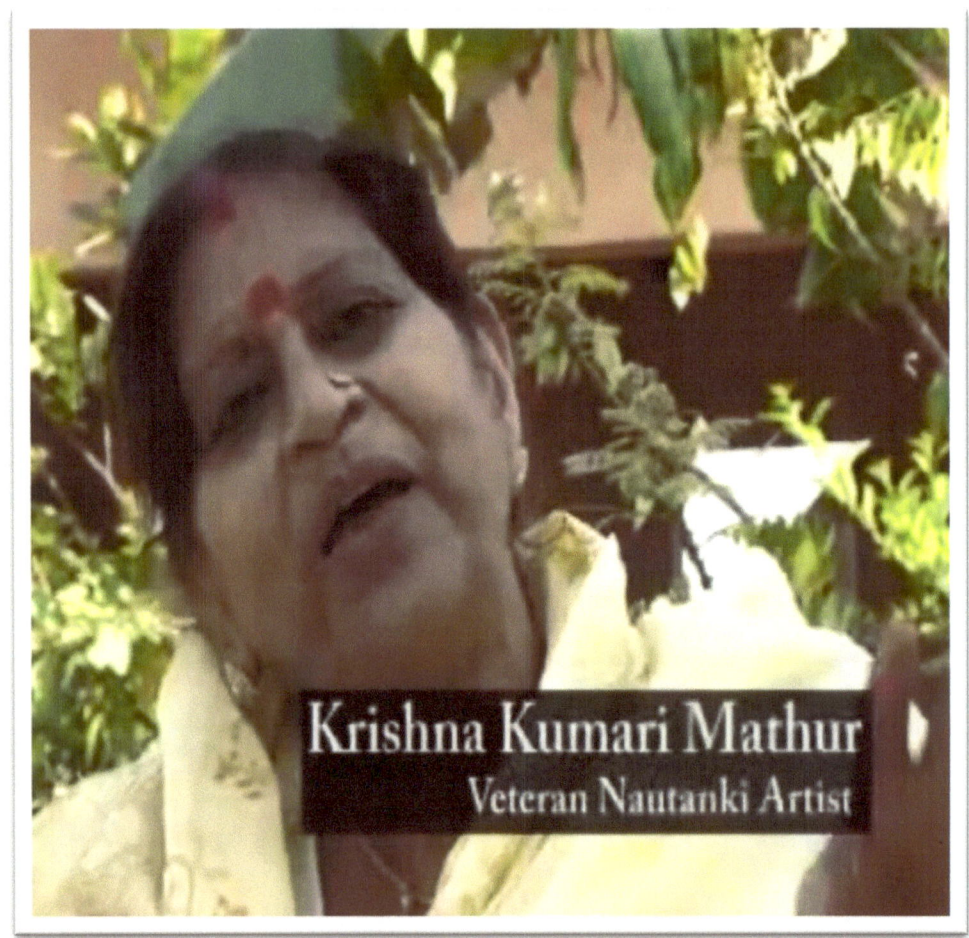

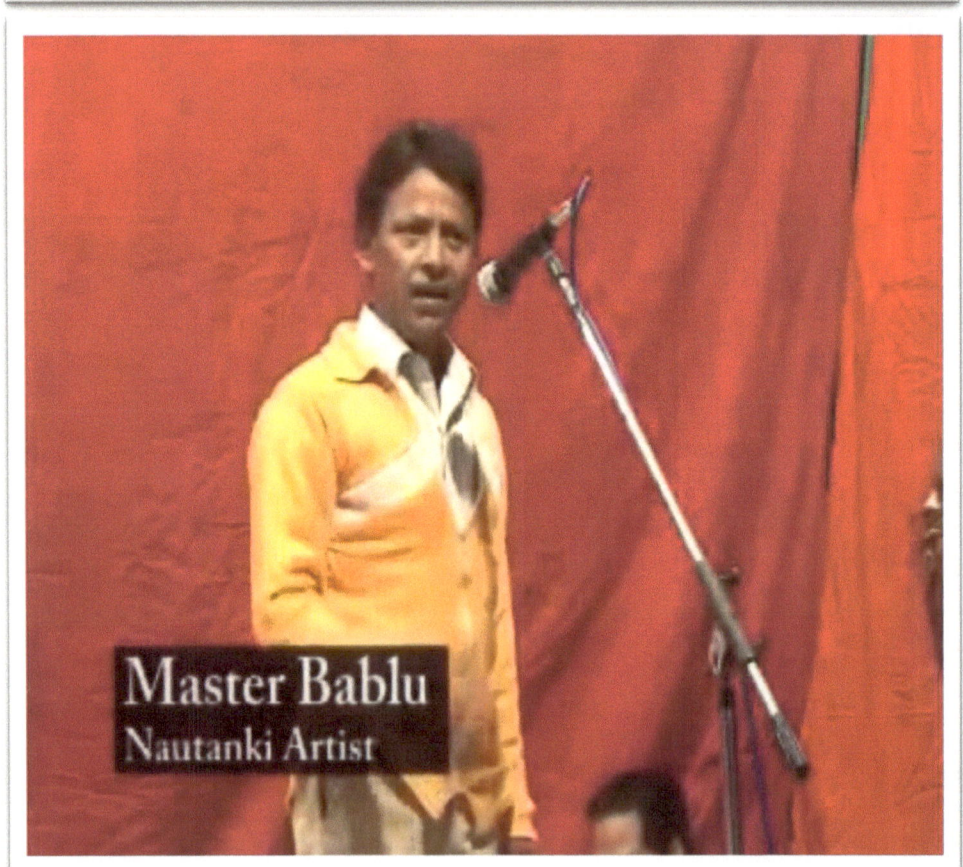

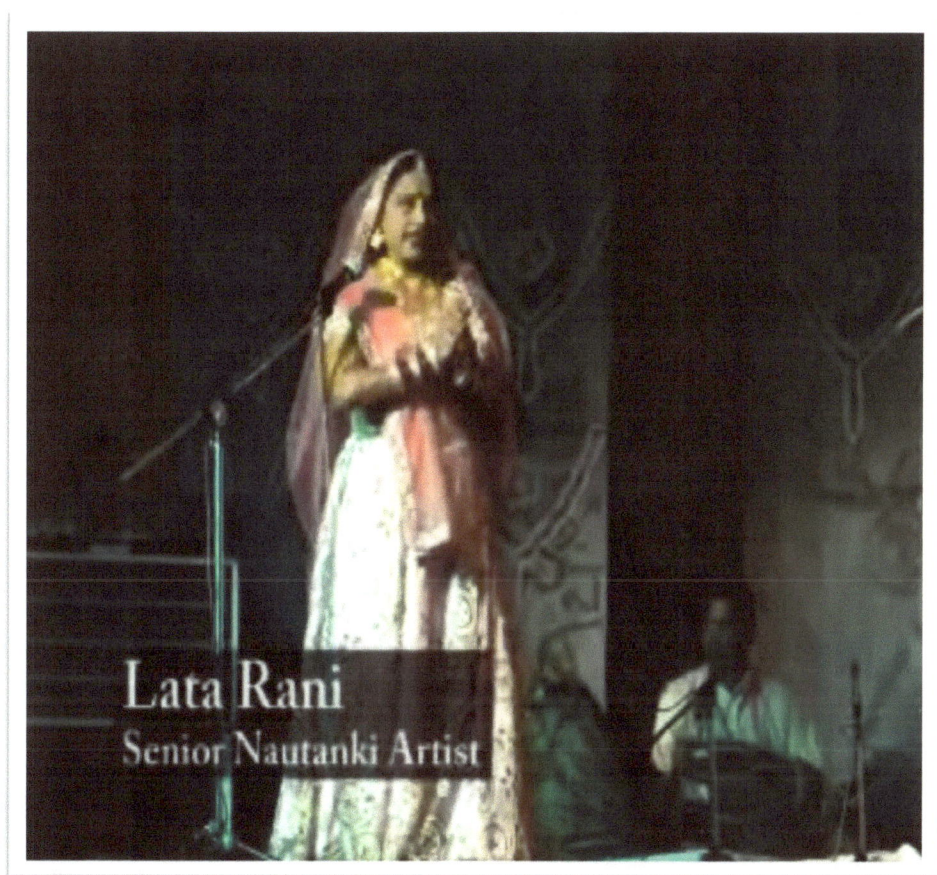

Lata Rani
Senior Nautanki Artist

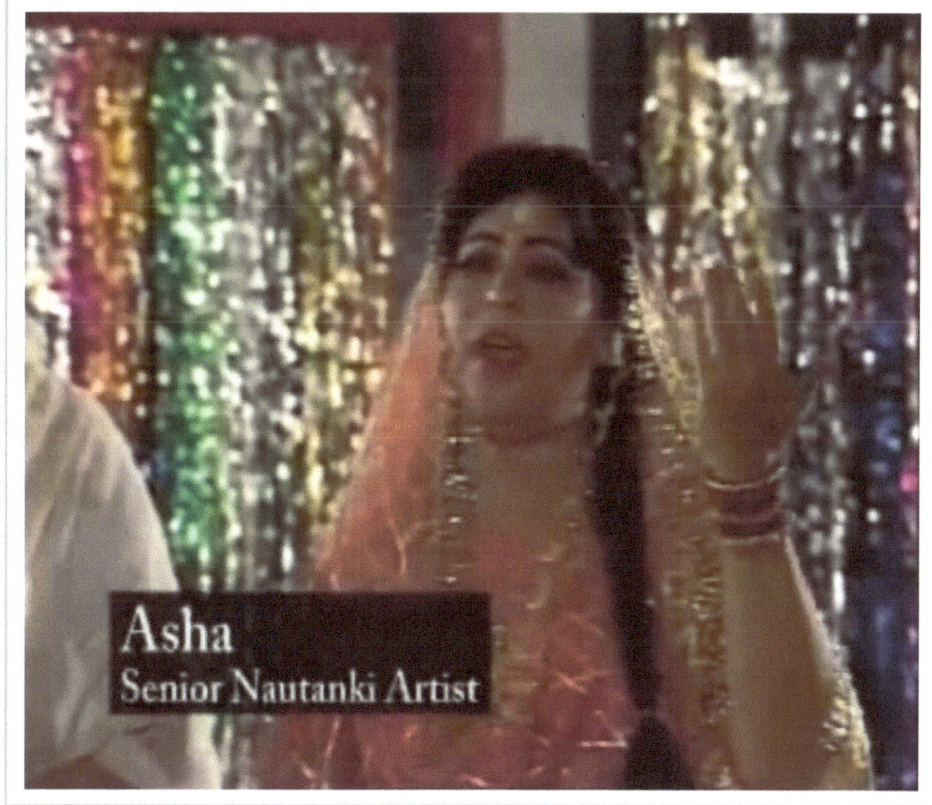

Asha
Senior Nautanki Artist

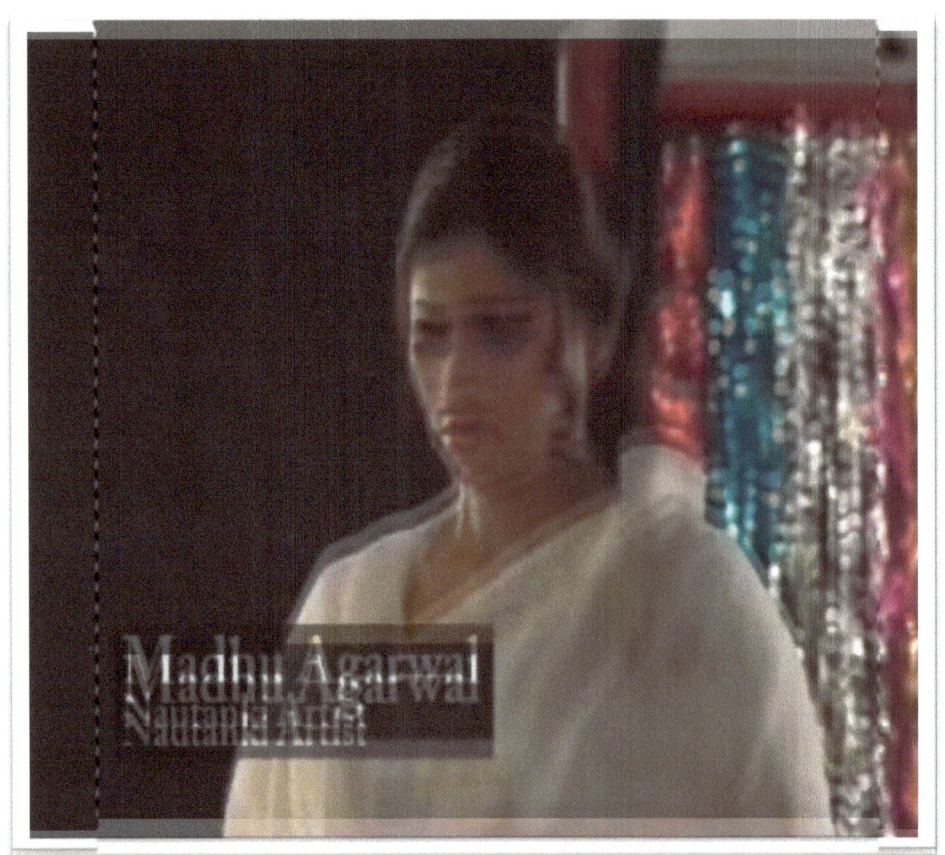

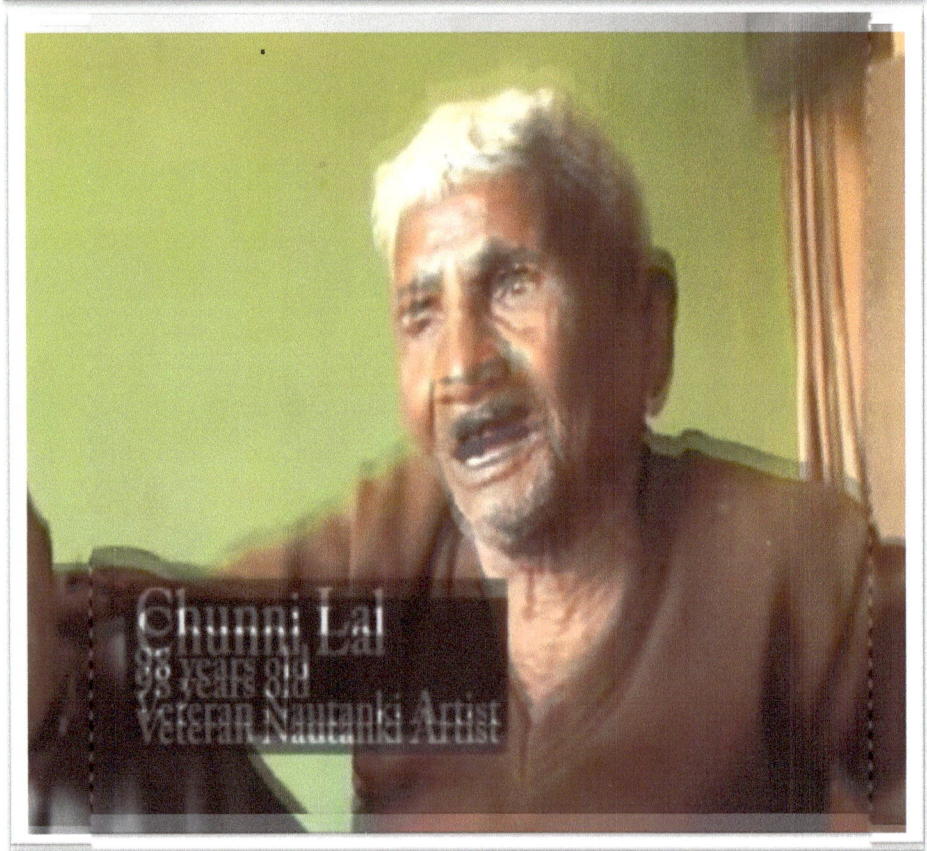

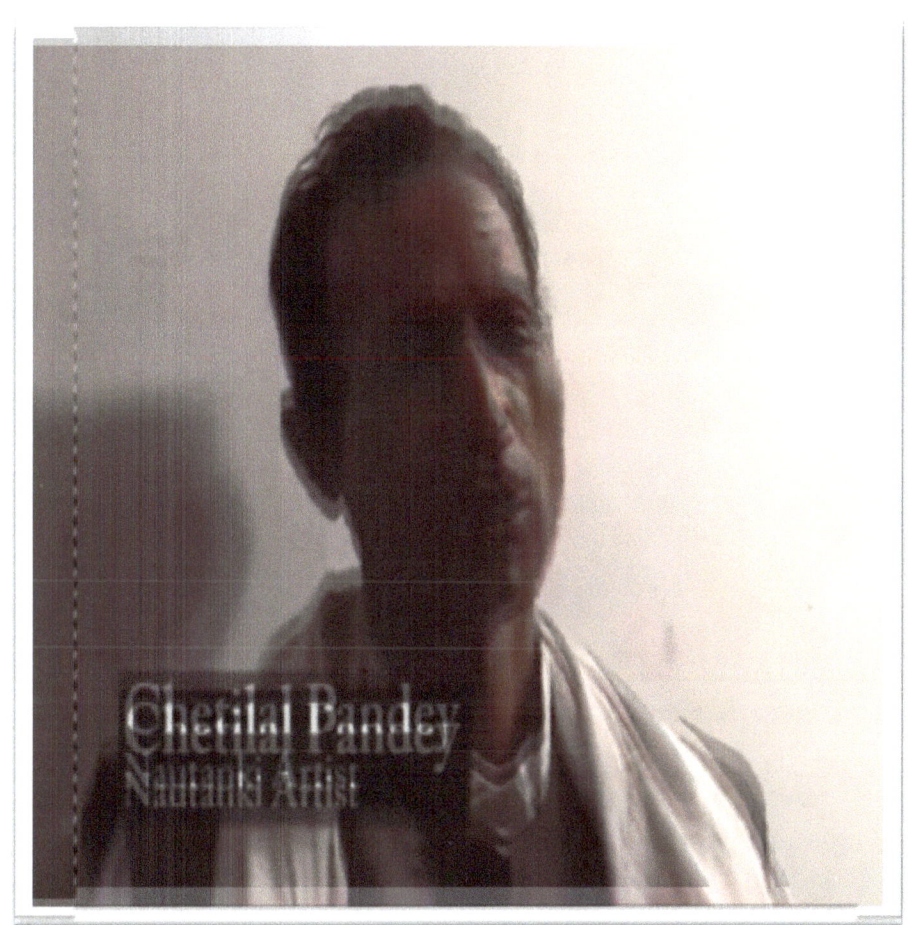
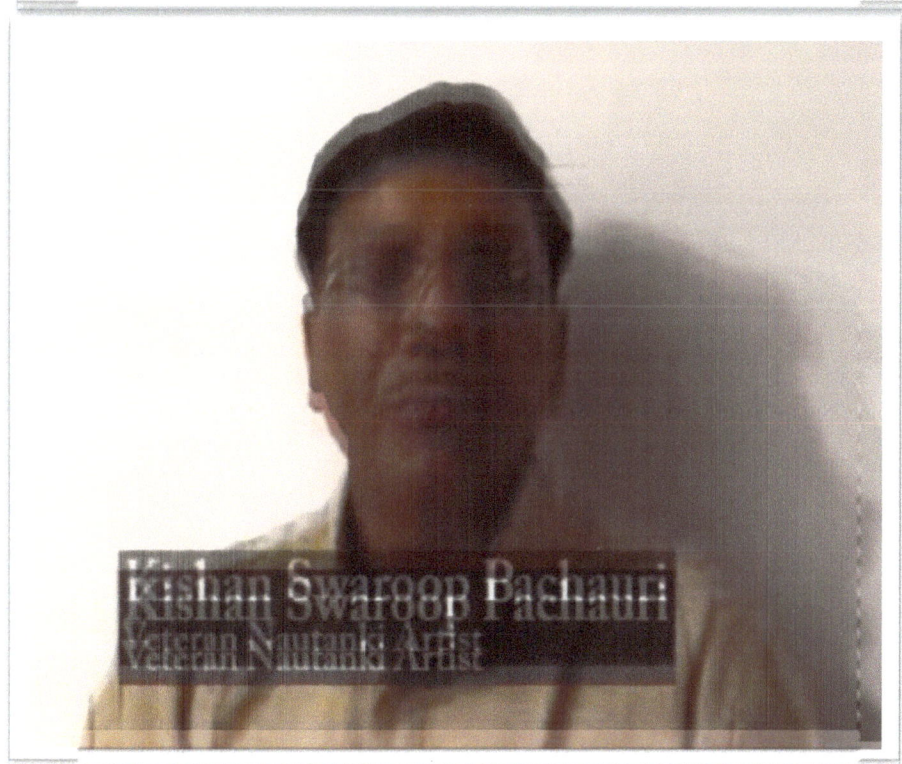

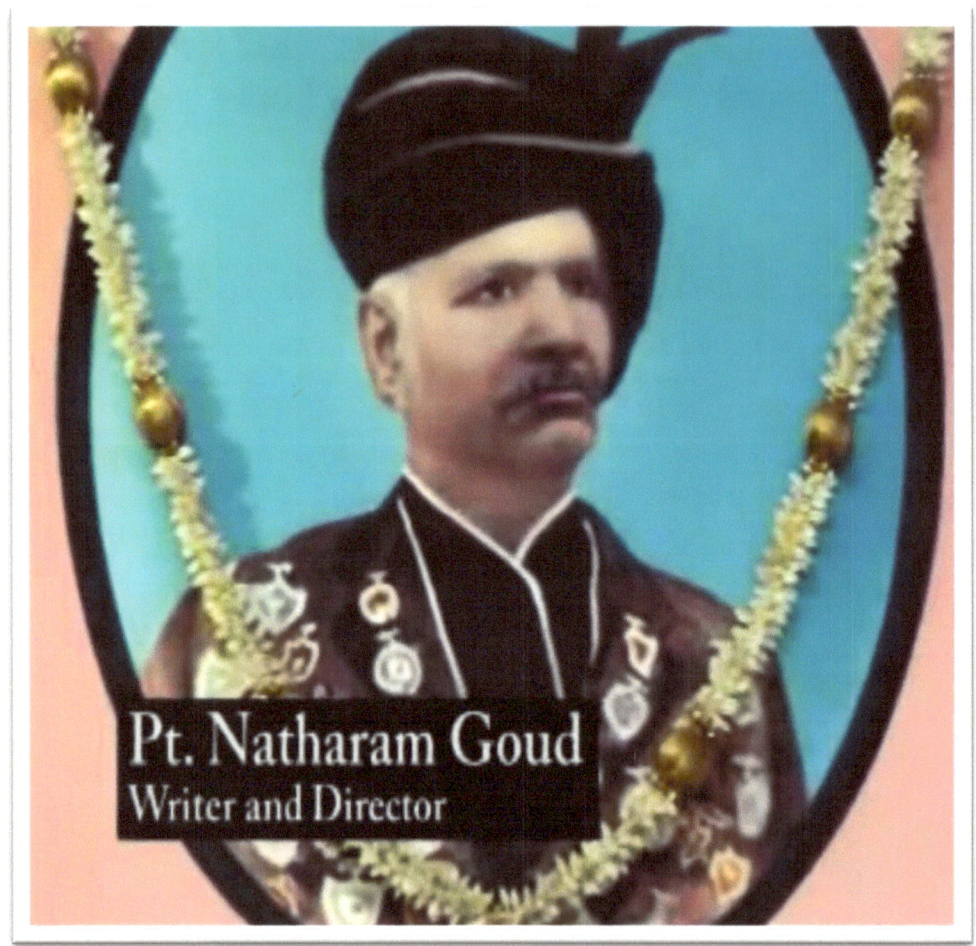

*(Figure:19-30 Veteran Nauṭankī Artists (Source:* The photographs developed from the video retrieved on 17/03/2016 from the web page:http://hooz.pk/watch/OwDYtbVYDS4)

The demand of the Nauṭankī artists depends on quality of the voice and the ability to draw the meaning of the dialogues and the ability to expression of the dialogues in histrionic representation.

The stories of the Nauṭankī plays are generally based on Mathology, Historical Narrations, Romance, folklore and contemporary issues.The language of Nauṭankī is mix of Rajasthani and other sub dialects. Like the śekhāwāṭī khyāla, Classical ragas are used in Nauṭankī with folk tunes.

Pt. Nāthaaram Gaud was famous *Writer and Director of folk Nauṭankī play such as* Vīrāṅganā Vīramatī alias Jagdev Kankali, Amar Singh Rāṭhaura alias āgare kī Laḍāī, Rūpa Basant alias Genda kī Corī, śravaṇa Caritra alias Dharma Patākā, Khudā Dosta alias Mohabbata ke āṁsū and Rājā Hariścandra.

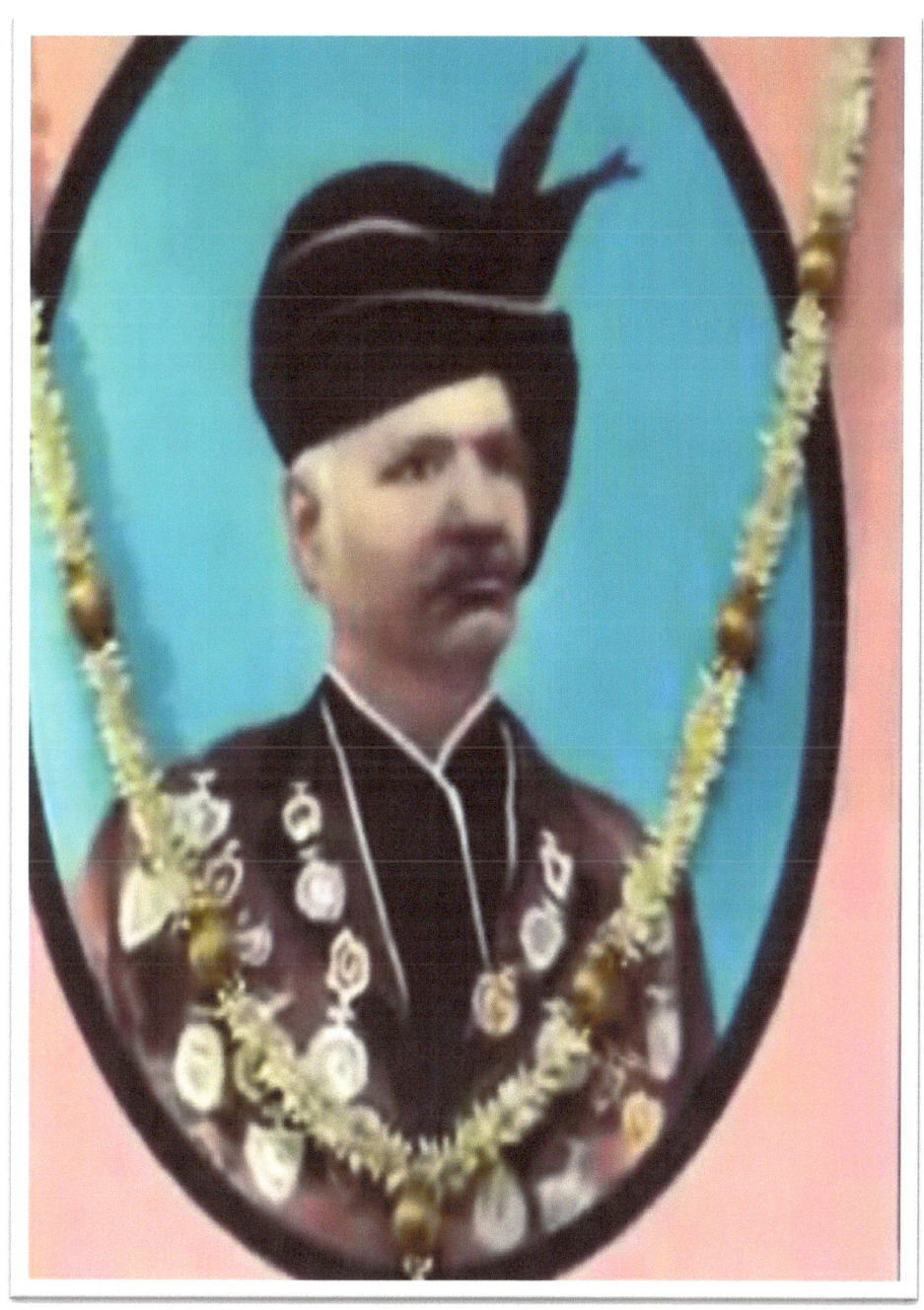

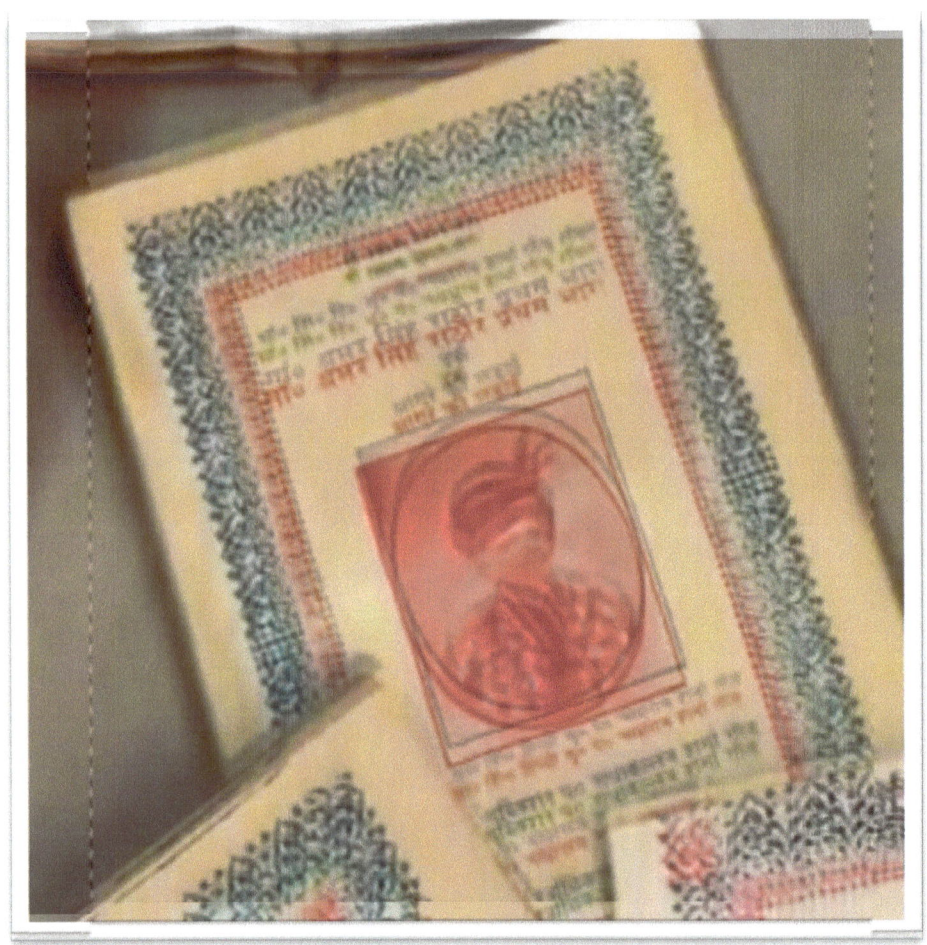

(Figure: 31-32 Late. Pt. Natharam Gaud, Writer and Director, Nauṭankī (Source: The photograph developed from the video retrieved on 17/03/2016 from the web page:http://hooz.pk/watch/OwDYtbVYDS4)

*"It is historically related to a number of other forms, generically called Swānga, and derives its particular name from a certain popular libretto: the story of Princess Nauṭankī, beloved of Phūla Singh, the younger brother of Bhūpa Singh."[3]*

Nauṭankī is dynamic traditions which have different new styles and themes according to the time. Nauṭankī have historical, literary and contemporary issues which are secular in nature in its plot. Some time we see that some Nauṭankī plays have incorporated with "vulgar" and "depraved" content but still

---

[3] Hansen, Kathryn; Grounds for play: the Nauṭankī theatre of North India, (ISBN-9780520072732), University of California press, Berkeley and Los Angeles, California, USA, December 1991.

Nauṭankī is in full swing in spite of the content coming from cinema and internet.

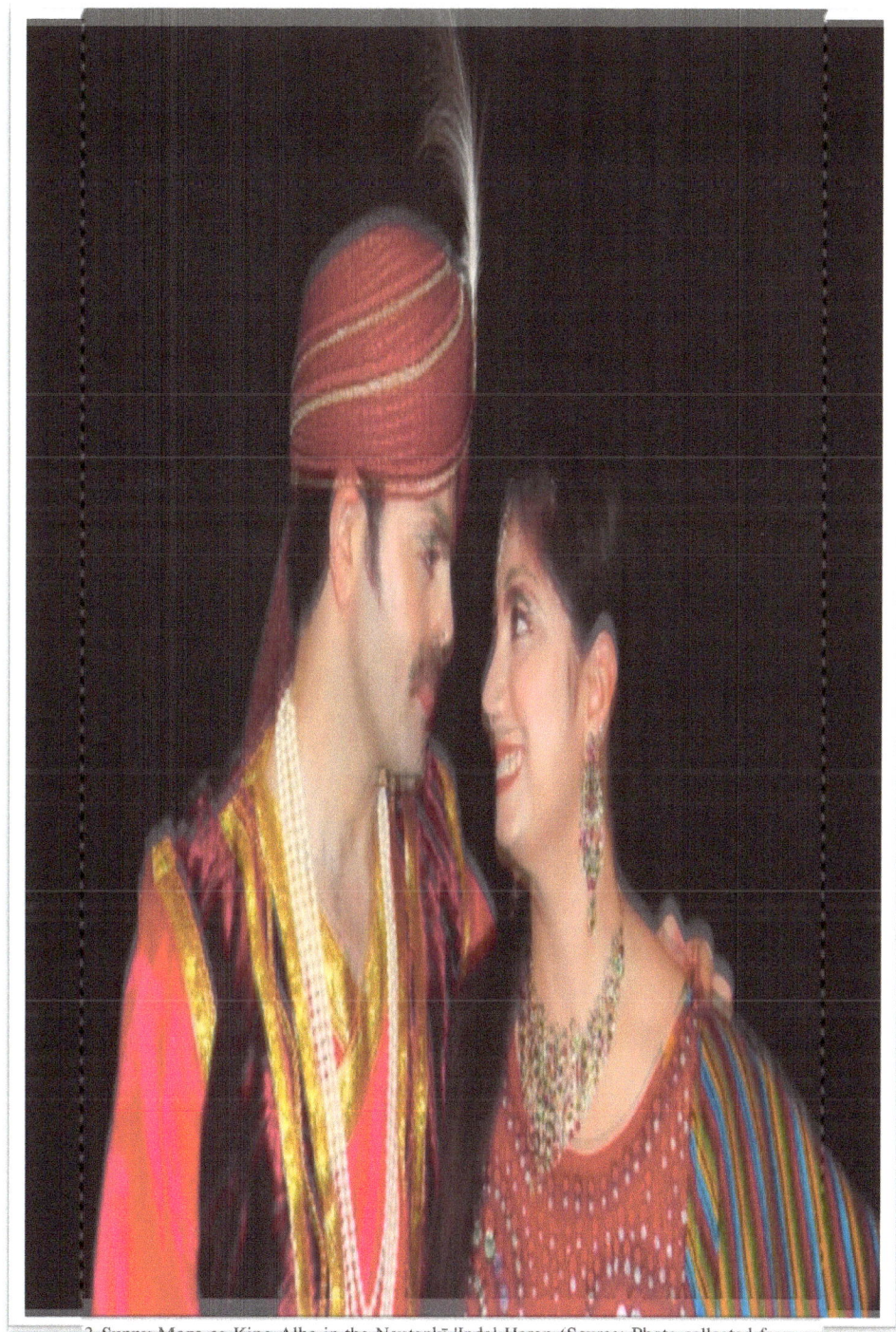

Figure : 33 Sunny Moza as King Alha in the Nauṭankī 'Indal-Haran (Source: Photo collected from google.com copy right free section retrieved on 17/03/2016)

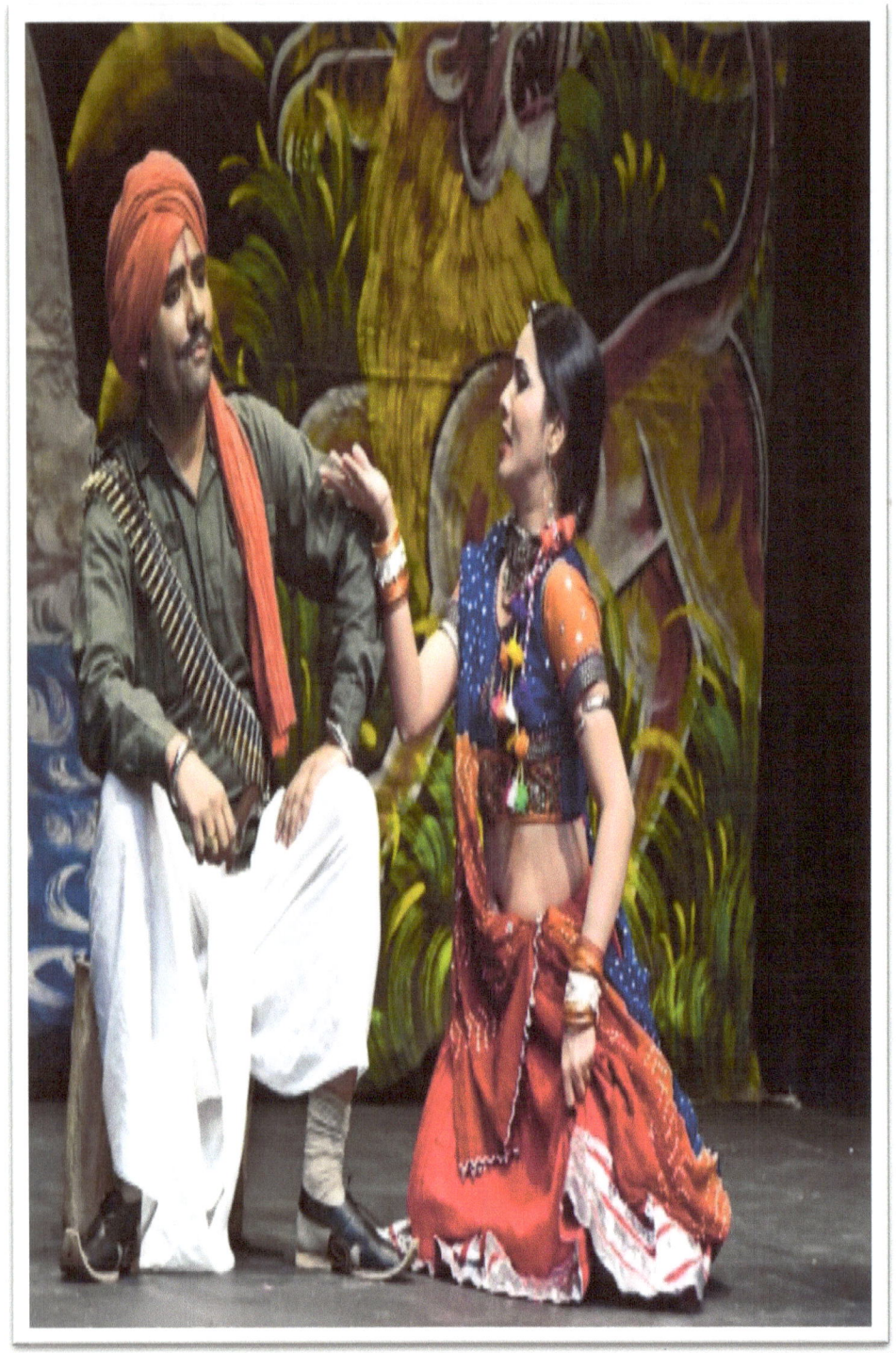

Figure:34  Dr. Devendra Sharma as Sultāna Ḍāku and Palak Joshi as Phūlakunwara in Nauṭankī "Sultāna Ḍāku"
(Source: google.com/copy right free section retrieved on 17/03/2016)

www.ingramcontent.com/pod-product-compliance
Lightning Source LLC
Chambersburg PA
CBHW051945210526
45473CB00006B/2387